DATE D D1445137

CHARLIE SIFFORD

Great Athletes

CHARLIE SIFFORD

Grant Britt

Greensboro

CHARLIE SIFFORD

Photos courtesy of

Personal Collection of Charlie and Rose Sifford
AP/Wide World Photos

Library of Congress Cataloging-in-Publication Data
Britt, Grant.
  Charlie Sifford / Grant Britt. —1st ed.
    p. cm. — (Great athletes)
  Includes bibliographical references (p. 62) and index.
  Summary: A biography of the man credited with breaking the racial barriers in
professional golf.
  ISBN 1-883846-27-7
    1. Sifford, Charlie, 1922- —Juvenile literature. 2. Golfers—United States—
Biography—Juvenile literature. 3. Afro-American golfers—Biography—Juvenile
literature. 4. Discrimination in sports—United States—Juvenile literature. [1. Sifford,
Charlie, 1922- . 2. Golfers. 3. Afro-Americans—Biography.] I. Title II. Series.
GV964.S53B75 1998
796.352 ' 092—dc21
[B]

Printed in the United States of America   97-48657
First Edition   CIP
                                                   AC

To my Mom
for all her love and support over the years,
wish you could have been here for this.

Contents

Charlie Sifford in 1948.

Chapter One

The year was 1940 and seventeen-year-old Charlie Sifford's life was about to change forever. It was a beautiful Monday morning in Charlotte, North Carolina, and Charlie set out to play a round of golf. Monday was caddie's day at the Carolina Country Club, the one day of the week when caddies were allowed to play the course. Charlie had been caddying for several years and was well liked by most of the club members. He had learned to play from watching members during their rounds. It was obvious he had a great talent, and a few of the members loaned him clubs occasionally.

Charlie had no idea anything was different on this day. All he had on his mind was a pleasant day on the course. But, before he could tee off, the resident golf pro ran up to him. "Charlie," he said, "we've got a little problem." Charlie tried to remember if he had pulled any pranks recently or said anything to any of the members that could cause trouble. He couldn't think of anything, but the expression on the pro's face told him it was serious. "You can't play here anymore," the pro said. "It's not that you've actually done anything, it's just that you can't be out here anymore. People have been saying things, and we think it's for your own good that you don't play here from now on." Charlie grew so angry he could hardly speak. It was the same old problem, his race. But this time Charlie took a little pride in the rejection. He knew that many of the white members had been growing jealous because he played the game so well. It bothered them to see a young African American out perform them in the most segregated of all sports.

Although Charlie took some satisfaction from making the club members envious of his talent, it was still a bitter loss. He enjoyed working on his game on the plush course. Charlie felt the old familiar anger well up inside. But, bitterly, he had no choice but to turn around and walk away.

At that moment Charlie knew he had to leave the segregated South. If he wanted to continue to develop as a golfer, he had to go some place where he would get the chance to play.

Charlie was not the only athlete to be hurt by racial laws that were still being enforced in 1940. Before there was a Tiger Woods in golf, or Arthur Ashe in tennis, or Jackie Robinson in baseball, being good at a sport did not mean a black athlete got a chance to play. The Brooklyn Dodgers did not give Jackie Robinson a chance until 1947. A black basketball player's best shot at professional ball was to play for the Harlem Globetrotters. Football was also dominated by white players and would remain that way for years.

The racial barrier in golf was especially hard to break. The sport was played mostly at country clubs, where whites controlled membership and blacks worked as cooks, waiters, janitors, or caddies. In the South, where it was often illegal for races to mix socially, it was almost impossible for a black man to have a career in golf.

Although unrecognized, African Americans had already made critical contributions to golf. In 1899, a black Boston dentist, Dr. George F. Grant, invented and patented the first golf tee. Until then, golfers hit tee shots off little mounds of sand. African American John Shippen, who gave lessons at a course in Long Island, New York, in the 1890s, is today recognized as being the first black golf pro. Shippen competed in five U.S. Opens and led the first tournament he entered for the first round, the first black man ever to accomplish this. His performance was hampered when the white players threatened to pull out if Shippen and a Native American player were allowed to continue playing. Thankfully, the president of the United States Golf Association, the forerunner of the PGA, stood firm, saying that he was going to let the tournament continue even if Shippen and the Native American were the only two players left. Shippen continued to contribute to the game by becoming the pro and greens keeper of the first black country club, The Shady Rest Country Club in New Jersey, where he worked for more than thirty years.

Charlie Sifford, who was to do more than anyone else

to bring down the color barrier in golf, was born in Charlotte, North Carolina, in 1922. Growing up, Charlie liked to do the things most boys his age did. He made the school baseball team as a catcher, but lost interest when a wild pitch took out two teeth. He tried boxing for a short time, but that just cost him more teeth and many more bruises. Then Charlie swung a golf club. He knew at that moment that he had discovered his sport.

Charlie's family lived near the Carolina Country Club, and many of his neighborhood friends caddied. They showed Charlie the ropes. A good caddie makes it his business to know the course. A serious player usually shows his appreciation for the caddie's help by tipping him. In the mid-thirties, in the heart of the Great Depression, when Charlie was growing up, money was in short supply. When Charlie discovered he could make money at golf, school took a back seat. Ten-year-old Charlie was earning a man's wage. He was grateful that he could earn his money doing something he liked. His father worked in a fertilizer plant, hauling one hundred-pound sacks on his shoulders.

But Charlie was not content to only carry someone else's golf clubs. He wanted to play and learned the game by studying the players. He didn't have money for lessons. After watching and learning, he either sneaked on the course or practiced on an open field next to the course. The most fun was on Mondays, caddie day.

Charlie soon discovered that he was a "natural." It takes hard work and constant practice, and patience, to be a good

John Shippen, who competed in the U.S. Open in the 1890s, was the first African American to play professional golf in the United States.

golfer. Charlie was willing to make the effort.

Then the golf pro told him that he could not play at the Carolina Country Club any longer. The pro tried to soften the blow by going to Charlie's parents and telling them that he thought the boy had the potential to make a living in golf. He told them that Charlie should be allowed to go and live with his uncle in Philadelphia. Because of the strict segregation laws in the South, Charlie would have more access to golf courses in the north. He could play on a regular basis. Charlie respected the pro for his efforts, but the blow still stung. In order to continue developing as a golfer, he would have to leave his family and friends behind.

Soon, however, events took the decision out of Charlie's hands. Charlie had a temper, and his frustration at the racist customs of the South had reached a boiling point. One day, a few weeks later, as Charlie walked into a neighborhood store to pick up groceries for his mother, the owner stopped him. The owner was a large man, an ex-wrestler, who was usually belligerent when drunk, as he was this day. "Hey little nigger," the man bellowed in Charlie's face, "Go tell my wife to come here."

Charlie decided to stand his ground. "You know me, sir, and you know my daddy won't put up with you talking to me like that."

"Shut your mouth, nigger, and do like I told you," the man said.

Charlie had had enough. "Call me that again," he said, "and I'm gonna go upside your head with a bottle!"

The man only became more belligerent. "Don't tell me what to do, you little n..." Whack! Before the man could finish the sentence, Charlie had made good on his threat. He hit the store owner so hard his forehead split open and he lost consciousness. Charlie ran home and told his parents what he had done. They immediately sent him to live with a family member in another part of town until things had cooled down.

Charlie was impatient, as usual, and after two weeks of staying at his aunt's he itched to play golf. He had not teed off the first hole before he was arrested. After making bail, he realized he would never beat the charges. He could spend the next few years in jail.

The decision to move to Philadelphia had been made when Charlie hit the drunken man with the bottle. Charlie's parents—with financial help from his friend the golf pro—bought him a ticket and put him on the first train to Philadelphia. Charlie Sifford had escaped the South, but, as he headed north, he had certainly not escaped racism.

Chapter Two

In Philadelphia, Charlie had no problem playing on the city course. But Philadelphia's winters were longer than the winters in Charlotte. He couldn't play in the winter. Charlie had to find another way to make a living. His uncle worked as a bricklayer and got Charlie a job helping him. Charlie soon discovered that hauling bricks in a wheelbarrow from dawn till dusk was not what he wanted to do. He got a job as a shipping clerk with the National Biscuit Company. Charlie worked there for the next three and a half years.

Charlie never forgot golf, however. Leaving work one day, in his first spring in Philadelphia, he saw a black man getting on a streetcar with a golf bag slung over his shoulder. Charlie knew the man from seeing him around the neighborhood, so he asked where he was going. "Cobb's Creek," said the man. Charlie tagged along and got his first look at Philadelphia's city golf course.

Although the city course was not as well laid out or maintained as the country club he was used to, it was challenging enough to sharpen Charlie's game. Charlie, however, wasn't yet as good a player as he thought he was. Harold Wheeler, who people considered to be the best golfer on the course, taught him that lesson. One day while watching Wheeler play a round, Charlie decided he could not see what all the fuss was about. Wheeler had a cross-handed grip, which made it look like he was hitting the ball with a backhand swing. Charlie became convinced Wheeler couldn't possibly hit the ball with any accuracy. He was sure he could beat him.

"Hey," said Charlie by way of introduction, "My name's Charlie Sifford, and I'm here to kick your butt."

Wheeler turned without a word, gesturing for Charlie to follow him onto the course. "How much you got to lose, kid?" he asked Charlie.

They decided to wager ten dollars on the first nine holes and ten dollars on the second nine.

At the end of the match, Charlie's money was gone. But before strolling off the green, Wheeler turned to Charlie and said, "Don't feel too bad, kid. You just got taken by the best golfer in the world."

Determined not to let that happen again, Charlie put money down on a set of decent clubs. Now he could work on his game full time. Within weeks, he saw an improvement in his game. He challenged Wheeler again and beat him, impressing him so much that from then on he and Charlie were partners, splitting the money they could hustle from other players. They soon earned a reputation and players came from all around to challenge them. They even took on Mike Souchak, who later played with Charlie on the Seniors Tour, and beat him.

America had entered World War II in 1941. Charlie was drafted in 1943 and, after basic training, sent to Okinawa. His job was to hit beaches soon after an invasion had taken place and to set-up communications. After the war ended in 1945, and before being discharged, Charlie formed a golf team.

Back in Philadelphia in 1946, Charlie began receiving invitations to play for bigger stakes. In 1946 he was invited to the National Negro Open. It was the largest black golf event in the country and was filled with famous amateur participants from all walks of life. At the tournament, he met boxers Joe Louis and Sugar Ray Robinson, and singing great Billy Eckstine. He also met Teddy Rhodes, the man many considered the best black golfer.

Although he did not win the tournament, Charlie ended with an acceptable score. He had been able to hold his own against the pros. Charlie decided he was ready for the big time. He didn't think to wonder if the big time was ready for him.

Charlie thought he was on his way to being a pro, but he still had things to learn. Golf does not involve a team. Players are not recruited, scouted, or drafted. There's no farm team system to bring you along. An aspiring golf pro has to do everything himself, unless he is lucky enough to get a sponsor—a company or individual that will finance his career. Charlie, of course, did not have a sponsor, or any

This group portrait was taken at a UGA tournament. Standing from the left are Charlie, middle-weight boxing great Sugar Ray Robinson, and Ted Rhodes, who Charlie believes was one of the greatest golfers ever.

prospects of finding one. No one was interested in funding a young black golfer.

There were two golf associations at the time. The Professional Golfers Association (PGA), which was white only, and the United Golf Association (UGA) for black golfers. The UGA was founded in 1926 by a group of black doctors from Washington, D.C. The first tournament was held at Mapledale Country Club in Boston, an all-black club. The UGA was not as well funded as the PGA, and did not have as many tournaments, but it did give black golfers a chance to earn a few dollars from the sport. Tournaments were usually held on city courses. The National Negro Open was the most prestigious tournament of the tour, much like the Masters in the PGA. Eventually, Charlie won the National Negro Open five straight times from 1952 to 1956.

The UGA, and its celebrity players like Joe Louis and jazz singer Billy Eckstine, brought the game of golf to the attention of blacks, encouraging them to play. Ironically, whites could play on the UGA tour, but blacks could not play on the PGA tour. In 1948, Teddy Rhodes and Bill Spiller, two leading black players, challenged the PGA in court for the right to join the PGA and won. But it was a hollow victory. After the ruling was announced, the PGA changed its policy of how players were allowed to enter tournaments. From then on, any matches sponsored by or affiliated with the PGA would be by invitation only. This left the selection of participants up to the individual country clubs hosting the events. Because most were held at whites-

Boxing great Joe Louis began the process of breaking down the barriers against black golfers participating in professional events.

only country clubs, there was little chance any would invite black golfers.

It was boxing great Joe Louis who finally broke the color barrier in golf. Hailed as the greatest boxer of his time, Louis was respected in the white community as well as the black. An avid golfer, Louis was determined to break the color barrier. He challenged the PGA in 1952 by announcing that he was going to play in the all-white San Diego Open. Louis knew the power his celebrity status had on the press and made sure that every contact he had with the PGA was well reported. Louis successfully forced their hand and the PGA said that he could play—but only because he had gotten a sponsor to back him. Two other black golfers who had applied to play with Louis were not let in, supposedly because no sponsors could be found for them. Louis played the tournament and later forced the board to vote on a resolution to allow black players to play in tournaments.

Once again, the PGA found a way around the ruling. It announced that black golfers could play in tournaments, but only if one of the ten sponsors for a tournament backed them, or if they could qualify for one of only ten open spots in a qualifying round against the best golfers in the world. An additional catch was that even if the African American players accomplished all these goals they were still not allowed to be members of the PGA. There was still a whites-only clause in the group's charter.

Charlie and a few of the best African American players began participating in some PGA events. Their entry was

Charlie was at the peak of his game in 1948, when this photo was taken.

determined by the attitudes of the people holding the tournament. Their reception was usually cold. But at the Los Angeles Open and the Canadian Open they usually received warm welcomes. Some of the white players, such as Sam Snead, treated them as equals. Others did their best to ignore them.

During this period, Charlie was becoming something of a legend on the UGA. Charlie was now playing with top-notch golfers and celebrities like Joe Louis. These famous people introduced him to their famous friends. Joe Louis was known for his generosity, and he liked Charlie. So when Joe's friend Billy Eckstine, who most people referred to as Mr. B., showed interest in golf but didn't have time to learn the game because he was on the road all the time, Louis suggested that Charlie become Eckstine's personal golf instructor. Both men agreed and started a partnership that was to last for ten years.

Charlie's duties included more than working as a personal golf trainer to Eckstine. He also took care of his clothes, made sure they got to the place where Eckstine would be performing that day, as well as running personal errands.

Charlie's most important duty for Mr.B. was finding golf matches with players willing to play for high stakes. When some local player challenged Mr.B. to play for big money, Eckstine answered: "Sure, but let me bring my friend along—he's not very good, but he likes to play." Charlie would dog it for a few holes, playing poorly, until the bets were raised. Then Charlie would play his best game.

Charlie worked for singer Billy Eckstine for ten years, serving as his golf teacher, personal valet, and traveling companion.

Eventually, Charlie became well known as Mr. B.'s hustler and had to use a fake name in order to find challengers.

All the playing Charlie did on the road did wonders for his game. He was now good enough to consistently be on the pro circuit. Money was not a problem, either. Eckstine was a very generous man. He readily paid Charlie's entry fees and expenses for him to enter tournaments.

Charlie was finally able to make his living playing golf, but not in the way he wanted. The only tournaments that paid enough to let him stop hustling for Mr. B. was the PGA. He knew his game was good enough to compete with the best. The only problem was the color of his skin. Charlie determined that it was time to change this.

Chapter Three

Charlie had another reason for wanting to break into the PGA. He had married Rose Crumbley, and they soon had a son, Charles Jr. Now living in California, family financial pressures were even more motivation for him to earn larger prizes. This did not stop Charlie from giving up his job with Mr. B. in order to focus all his attention on golf.

In the winter of 1957, Charlie decided to enter the Long Beach Open. California did not discriminate as openly as other states against black players, so Charlie had managed to make some pretty good money out there. He met little resistance to his entry and was determined to make a good showing.

Charlie started out the last day of the tournament with a bang. Shooting a birdie on the first hole, one shot under par, he made par on the second, got another birdie on the third, birdied the next two holes, and shot a par on the next. At this point he was four under par and was in the running for the lead. He kept up the pace all the way to the seventeenth hole where he missed a putt. He was now tied with Eric Monti for the lead, with one hole to go.

Eighteen was a 475-yard par five. Charlie blew his second shot and fell short of the green. His third shot got him within striking distance, and he birdied the hole. He now had the lead in a major PGA tournament—the first black man ever to hold that honor. But he couldn't start celebrating yet—everything was riding on Monti's putt. The crowd was quiet as Monti stepped up to the ball, studied it carefully, and then tapped in his ten-foot putt for the tie.

The phrase "sudden death"—where players play until someone wins a hole—had never seemed so appropriate. Everything Charlie had worked for his whole life was riding on what he did in the next few minutes. The pressure on him was enormous. Charlie reached down deep and played the best golf of his life. But Monti was a worthy opponent. They tied the first hole of the sudden death. On the second, Charlie missed an easy putt. But luck was with Charlie—Monti missed an equally easy putt. They were still tied.

Charlie knew he couldn't count on such luck any longer. If he wanted to win he'd have to do something about it himself. On the third hole, Monti teed off first and made par on the hole. Charlie needed a birdie to win. He let fly with a beautiful drive that landed within feet of the cup. If he sunk the putt he would win. After taking a deep breath and saying a silent prayer, Charlie sunk the putt. He was the first black man to win a tournament on the PGA tour.

Charlie had made his presence known on the PGA. His victory at Long Beach by no means guaranteed his acceptance as a full member of the PGA, however. His win earned

This photo of Charlie was published in papers all over the country after he won the 1957 Long Beach Open.

him nationwide recognition, but he soon found out that everything else was the same. The PGA still would not let him join the organization.

The main legal obstacle to his membership was an item in the PGA charter called the Caucasian clause. One little sentence stated simply that the tour was open to Caucasians only. Oddly enough, the clause had not been entered into the charter by Southerners. It was the work of some members from Michigan, whose argument was that no black person had ever started or maintained a "good" golf or "country" club. Therefore, they should not be allowed to play in one established by whites.

Charlie's win at the Long Beach tournament started a movement to get the clause changed, but it wouldn't happen right away. It would be several more years before he could make a decent living playing the game he loved.

At this critical time, Charlie again got help from his friend Mr. B. The attorney general of California was a golfing buddy of Eckstine's. When he was first told of the rule he was horrified. "You mean to tell me that this national organization actually has it written down that a black man cannot join their organization?" the attorney general asked.

The attorney general took on the PGA immediately. First, he had to get PGA officials to admit that they had such a rule. Next, he told them that they were breaking California state law. His office would have no choice but to block all of their tournaments in the state if they did not remove the clause from their constitution. The PGA gave in—or seemed to. In 1960, Charlie, as a resident of California, finally got his membership in the PGA

But the California attorney general did not have the power to make other states vote on or approve the removal of the rule. It soon became clear that the PGA had no intention of letting black players participate on an equal level with whites. Although Charlie had a card and could technically play in all PGA tournaments, it was up to the PGA in the individual states to decide whether Charlie would be allowed to play there. This was critical because the PGA had another rule that said for a golfer to actually be a member of its organization he had to play in twenty-five tournaments a year for five consecutive years.

The catch was soon clear. Charlie couldn't play in many states because of the Caucasian clause. This meant competing in twenty-five tournaments a year was almost impossible. Therefore, he would not be able to hold on to his membership. Again, the PGA had given with one hand and taken away with the other.

The attorney general's action in California had focused nationwide attention on the PGA, however. Now the National Association for the Advancement of Colored People (NAACP) became interested in the case and started to ask some rather disturbing questions. For example, if a man had the qualifications, talent, and dedication to excel at his sport, why was he being denied a chance to play?

The focus of the NAACP brought on national attention. The PGA began to wilt. In 1961, thanks to the continued efforts of California's attorney general and the NAACP, the PGA finally dropped the Caucasian clause nationwide.

Now Charlie had other hurdles to clear. He was no longer excluded from the tour, but he was still not a member. He had to "earn" his card. To qualify, he had to be sponsored by a country club pro, or to have been employed as a pro or assistant pro for five years. In addition, he needed two PGA members who were willing to sponsor him and to keep his game at the high level necessary to qualify to play in at least twenty-five tournaments a year. These were almost impossible conditions for a black man, who had been denied access to country clubs and the PGA his entire career. It would be three more years before Charlie could play in enough tournaments to satisfy the PGA that he was a "real" pro golfer. He was determined to try, however. Charlie Sifford was now forty-one years old and beginning his golf career over as a rookie.

Chapter Four

One of the first tournaments Charlie entered after the Caucasian clause was dropped was the 1961 Greater Greensboro Open. After the first day, Charlie led with a score of three under par. Walking off the course that afternoon, he felt the pressure of being the first and only African American playing in a tournament in the South—and of being in the lead.

Charlie had been surprised to receive an invitation to Greensboro, North Carolina. Three years earlier, a group of black men trying to play on a Greensboro city golf course had been arrested for trespassing. The men were found not guilty, but then the course hired a private company to run the course, and officials had once again excluded blacks from play. Greensboro did not seem like the type of city willing to break tradition in sports. But, unknown to him, Charlie had some help working behind the scenes in Greensboro. The president of the local chapter of the NAACP had connections with the membership committee of the GGO and had used his influence to get Charlie an invitation to the tournament.

Later that night, after the first round, Charlie had finally begun to relax. He was staying at a friend's house, and as he prepared to go to bed the phone rang. An anonymous caller threatened to kill him if he showed up for play the following day. Charlie, determined to not let the bigot intimidate him, angrily gave the caller his tee time.

The next morning, Charlie teed off as scheduled. Nobody tried to kill him, but a large group of young white men followed him around for fourteen holes. They yelled racial slurs at him inches from his face before police eventually removed them. The fact that the group was allowed to harass him for that length of time without anything being done about it hurt Charlie's concentration. At the end of that day, he was third in the standings.

When the tournament was over, no one connected with it had apologized for, or even commented on, the verbal assault. Charlie dropped to fourth place.

After Greensboro, Charlie knew that the odds were against him. His troubles on the tour were just beginning. He was determined to make a living playing golf, and nothing anybody said or did was going to change his mind.

Charlie's next tournament was in Texas. He drove all the way down to find out after he arrived that he'd been denied entry. The sponsors didn't want him to play. It was that simple, and there was no arguing with it. It seemed that whatever Charlie did was not good enough. The whites-only rule might be off the books, but the attitude was still firmly in place.

This photo was taken on the first day of the 1961 GGO, when Charlie earned a three stroke lead.

The same thing happened at the next tournament, and the one after that. Charlie finally decided that he would not yet be allowed to play in most tournaments held in the South. In order to keep up his game and to earn his membership qualifications, he began playing everywhere he could outside the south. He traveled all over the country to play golf.

While the sponsors tried to keep Charlie out of their tournaments, some fellow golfers were supportive and sympathetic to Charlie's troubles. Once, four years after his appearance at the Greater Greensboro Open, Charlie was in Florida for a tournament. When he sat down for breakfast in the club dining room, an official came to his table and told him that he had to go elsewhere to eat. Charlie's fork stopped in midair, a chunk of egg sliding unnoticed to his plate. He felt the old, familiar anger rise up inside. But, as he thought about a reply, he realized that nothing he could say would do any good. He slowly stood up and walked out of the room with his breakfast in his hand.

Charlie decided to eat in the locker room. As he sat down, he heard the sound of cleats on the tile floor. Three of the white golfers on the tour, carrying their breakfasts, sat down without saying a word and began to eat. From then on, whenever Charlie had to eat in the locker room, he didn't have to eat alone.

Charlie appreciated the support the few courageous white players, such as Sam Snead and Gary Player, were willing to give him. It helped him maintain his morale. The fight, however, did not get easier. Occasionally, a country

Golfing legend Sam Snead was one of the white players who always treated Charlie with respect.

club would alter its rules and let him play in a tournament, but using the locker room to change clothes was off-limits. Charlie would have to change his shoes in the parking lot and go directly to the first tee.

Other places went to whatever extreme necessary to keep him from competing. In 1964, when he entered a tournament in Mobile, Alabama, the event was cancelled to keep him from participating.

Throughout the 1960s, Charlie grew more and more angry at the treatment he received. All he wanted was to be allowed to play golf at the level he was capable of competing. He knew he was one of the best golfers in the nation. White players did not have to deal with the increased hassles and pressures of not being allowed to eat in the dining room or dress in the locker room. They did not find human excrement waiting for them in the holes, or have to focus on a shot while the white spectators were mouthing obscenities or giving him that cold, mean look he grew so used to seeing.

Sometimes the pressure got to Charlie and it showed. He would chew the cigar he kept always clamped between his teeth. Sometimes he refused to smile and act gracious to the very people responsible for the rules that held him down. When reporters asked him what he thought of some injustice, he expressed his honest opinion in blunt language. Soon, he had a reputation as an angry man. This image as angry and aggressive has followed Charlie his entire life. It provided a handy label to those who wanted to attack him for breaking down golf's racial barriers. Charlie saw it as the inevitable backlash against him. White people always thought black people who fought back against discrimination were angry and disruptive. He just wanted to play golf and was determined to do what it took to fight for that right. They could think of him what they liked.

Chapter Five

Charlie continued playing on the PGA tour during the decade of the 1960s. Despite all the conditions that made his life difficult, he usually finished the year in the top twenty-five money winners. In 1964 he finally earned his membership in the PGA. But the big-money wins eluded him. He won the Canadian Open in 1962, but failed to win any of the larger tournaments for the next five years. He played well enough to hold on to his card and to earn enough money to support his family and to meet his expenses. He tried to not grow bitter because so many of his best playing years had been spent fighting to gain entry onto the tour.

As 1967 began, Charlie determined to try even harder. His second son, Craig, had been born the year before. He was in his mid-forties. It was time to make his last attempt to raise the level of his game. More than anything else, he wanted to win a big tournament. He buckled down for one last run at achieving a win in a major tournament.

Charlie started the year with a good showing at the Greater Greensboro Open, coming in fifth. By late summer, he had made more money than he had since joining the tour. He entered the Hartford Open with high hopes. The purse, $20,000, was large for the time. Charlie felt like it was his time to claim it.

The first day of competition, Charlie ended up fifth in a strong field, including Lee Trevino, Gary Player, and Gene Littler. By the end of the second day, Charlie had slipped to fifteenth and was looking up at a long line of players listed above him on the board.

On the third day, Charlie began to make his move. He was in twelfth place by Sunday. Entering the last day of the tournament, it was time to turn on the heat. At the end of nine holes, Charlie was two under par. This was a fine round of golf. Charlie was in the running.

At the thirteenth hole, Charlie was four under for the day. His tee shot took off like a rocket, hooked sharply into a bunker, exploded out, and was stopped by the tall grass in the rough. The ball was less than thirty feet from the cup. But because of the difficulty in putting in the rough it might as well have been a mile. He would have to chip—a shot that tried to get under the ball and let it fly the few feet to the hole—and hope for the best. Charlie concentrated and . . . chipped the ball into the cup for an eagle, which is two shots under par. He was now six under for the match. The pressure was building.

Charlie was hot, but his competition was smoking along right behind him. There was no room for error. The next two holes, sixteen and seventeen, had been troublesome for him every round of the tournament. Today he birdied the six-teenth to take the lead. But the seventeenth was the one he really worried about. He managed to par the hole, keeping alive his lead of seven under.

By now the gallery had gotten wind of what was going on, and the final hole, the eighteenth, was jam-packed with spectators. Charlie steadied his trembling knees and hit his tee shot straight down the middle of the fairway. On the second shot the pressure got to him. The ball flew right into the bunker.

All was not lost, however. Because the hole was a par four, he could still win—if his next two shots were perfect. Trying not to think about what was riding on his next move, Charlie took out his sand wedge and chipped a beautiful shot that rolled to within four feet of the hole. As a hush fell over the crowd, Charlie took a deep breath, hunkered down, and tapped the ball firmly into the cup for the win!

There were no shouts of "nigger" or "darkie" now. The late summer afternoon air was filled with one continuous joyful roar from a crowd applauding a great round of golf.

This win at the Hartford Open qualified Charlie for the Masters, held in Augusta, Georgia. The Masters is consid-ered golf's most important tournament, its ultimate chal-lenge. However, the group that runs the match considers itself independent from the PGA and is not bound by its rules. In the 1960s, the Masters was proud of the one thing it insisted would never change—there had never been a black player in the tournament. The chairman of the Masters

Charlie won the 1967 Hartford Open by playing some of the best golf of his career.

said proudly: "As long as I live, there will be nothing at the Masters but white players." It would be ten more long years before the Masters would allow blacks to play, even though Charlie had first been made eligible, if he had been white, by his 1962 win at the Canadian Open, and again in 1967 when he won the Hartford Open. But Charlie was dismissed out of hand both times.

The official reason for the discrimination, according to Clifford Roberts, who ran the event, was that he had been told that "if a Negro ever got into the Masters, there would be no more tournament." The Masters maintained this strict racial discrimination by twisting the rules. There were various ways a golfer could supposedly get into the Masters.

Any PGA member who won a major tournament during the year was invited. But after Charlie won the 1962 Canadian Open, the Masters committee announced that it would not be inviting the winner of the Canadian Open. The top twenty-five money winners were eligible, unless you were black. There was also rule thirteen: "One player, not otherwise eligible, either amateur or professional, can be selected by a ballot of former Masters champions." But in all the years Charlie played, not one of his fellow white golfers was brave enough to award him that honor.

The Masters was successful in denying Charlie entry after his 1967 Hartford Open victory. Masters officials were able to maintain their resistance to integrated sports throughout the 1960s.

Things began to change in 1970 when Lee Trevino, who was of Mexican heritage, announced publicly that the Masters "was not my kind of course. They can invite me all they want, but I'm not going there anymore."

The PGA tried to convince Trevino to take back his statement or to apologize. But, as a dark-skinned man, Trevino felt he had been treated rudely at the event and would not return. Although he qualified again in 1974, he again refused to attend.

The Masters experienced more uncomfortable publicity when South African Gary Player entered the tournament. Player was white, but he had a black caddie. Death threats were made and armed guards were hired to go around the course with Player.

Lee Trevino boycotted the Masters because of its discriminatory policies toward African Americans.

In 1975, Lee Elder became the first African American to compete in the Masters.

By 1973, there were still no blacks invited to the Masters. Eighteen congressmen began pressuring Masters Chairman Roberts to invite blacks, but Roberts held firm, saying that no blacks had qualified.

In 1975, Lee Elder became the first African American to play the Masters. By this time Charlie's best playing years were behind him and he was never invited to the Masters. This was just another of the opportunities denied to him because of his race.

Chapter Six

Charlie started 1969 by entering one of his favorite tournaments, the Los Angeles Open. Los Angeles was now his home town, and this had been one of the first PGA events he had participated in back in the 1950s. At the end of the first round he had shot a 63 and was leading a field that included Arnold Palmer and Lee Trevino, two of the hottest golfers of the era.

Charlie played some of the best golf of his life in the next two days to hold on to the lead. The last day settled into an intense competition between him and the man he was paired with that day, Harold Henning.

Charlie and Henning switched the lead between them throughout the day. Going into the last two holes they were tied and remained tied to the end. The playoff started on the fifteenth hole. Henning made par. Charlie's drive landed three feet from the hole. If he made the birdie putt, the $20,000 first place check was his. Charlie made the putt. The hometown gallery erupted into cheers.

Charlie had won another large tournament. Maybe now

he would receive some offers to endorse golf products. Professional athletes often make more money from endorsement contracts than from their sport. An endorsement contract means a company is willing to pay for the golfer to wear their clothes or to use their equipment, and to make commercials promoting their products on television and in magazines. Charlie's only opportunity to endorse a product had come early in his career. One small company came out with a line of Charlie Sifford clubs. The idea was to sell the clubs to the African American golfers. But, few stores were willing to stock the clubs. Charlie eventually bought the man's entire stock and sold them from the trunk of his car for several years.

Even after Charlie established himself on the tour and won a major tournament, no companies stepped forward to give Charlie a job as their spokesman. Some gave him shoes, gloves, pants and shirts, but they didn't ask him to talk about them or to appear in magazines or on television. He also got free clubs, balls, and bags occasionally, but again, nobody wanted Charlie to speak publicly for them. One company actually supplied him with cars for years without asking for his endorsement. Charlie, being the proud man that he was, refused to ask for the contracts. He did not have an agent to work behind the scenes for him like athletes of today do. He made too little money to give any to an agent.

Charlie got by on his own, but it hurt to see white golfers, many younger and without the wins he had under his belt, wearing beautiful clothes and driving fancy cars and getting paid to talk about them. But just like all the other abuse and intolerance that had been directed his way over the years, Charlie tried to shrug it off—he had a game to play.

By 1972, Charlie was fifty. His game was starting to slow down. It angered him to think of how many of his best years had been wasted trying to get on the tour. His lifetime earnings in golf were a little over $300,000, and it was getting more difficult for him to earn enough to stay alive. The size of the winner's purse had gotten bigger, but the rules on how the money was distributed had changed. A first place finisher could get as much as $60,000. The golfer who finished further down the list may only get a few hundred dollars. As his game tapered off, Charlie more and more often ended up leaving tournaments with barely enough money to cover his expenses. It was time to look for another way to make a living.

Golf was all Charlie knew how to do. He began to call the friends he had made over the years. But once again, doors slammed in his face. He got in touch with every club he had ever played, asking for any type of job related to golf that would help him support his family, but no country club was willing to hire him.

Finally, late in 1975, Charlie got a job offer. The Sleepy Hollow Country Club in Ohio was looking for a pro and was willing to consider Charlie for one reason. A formerly all-white private club opening itself to the public, it had to let everyone in, regardless of race or religion. Club officials

Rose Sifford and Charlie celebrating his victory at the 1969 L.A. Open.

wanted Charlie to be their symbol of how they had changed. Although he hesitated, it was the only job anyone had offered him. Charlie had no choice but to take it.

When he arrived at the Sleepy Hollow Country Club, the management said it didn't have the money to pay a big salary. He would have to earn his money from the pro shop. Charlie had to put up his own money to buy the stuff he sold in the pro shop. Charlie stuck it out for thirteen years, playing in whatever tournaments he could find to add to his income.

Even at this late stage, golf remained mostly whites-only. There was a once-a-year event called the PGA Seniors Championship held for golfers over fifty who had been on the tour, a forerunner of today's Seniors Tour. In 1976 Charlie won the event. The PGA had previously announced that the winner of the tournament would play against the winner of the British Senior Championship at a course to be selected by the PGA.

The PGA selected the Bide-a-wee Country Club in Portsmouth, Virginia. Not only was this club segregated; there had never even been a black caddie on the course. Nobody bothered to tell Charlie that information. This made him so mad that it threw his game off and he lost to the British player.

When the PGA created the Legends of Golf Tournament, it decided that participation would be determined by invitation only. This meant tournament officials could invite whomever they wanted, regardless of their qualifications or money earned over the course of their career. Players with fewer wins than Charlie were invited. He was not invited. When Charlie complained publicly, the director of the tournament told the press that Charlie Sifford was not a legend, therefore there was no reason to invite him.

The PGA shut him out the next year. When the press called each year to ask why he wasn't playing, he told them: "I don't know—why don't you ask them? It's not fair." In 1981, as the PGA worked to gain support for the newly created Seniors Tour, it announced that past winners of PGA Seniors Championships were invited to the Legends of Golf Tournament. Now they had to let Charlie play.

But the PGA had made its point. African American

Jim Dent is one of the golfers who benefited from Charlie's struggle to break the racial barrier in golf.

golfers such as Lee Elder and Jim Dent were playing the tour regularly by the late 1970s. But Charlie had been the one who broke the barriers. This fact reserved him a special place. The PGA seemed unwilling to ever forgive him.

In 1981, another tournament for senior golfers started up. It was called the Vintage, and it supposedly represented the best of golf's older players. By this time, Charlie had begun playing on the Seniors Tour regularly and was high on the list of top money winners and had won several major tournaments. He clearly expected an invitation. Once again he was disappointed. This time the excuse was that it was a pro-am tournament and the tournament managers thought black players would make the amateurs nervous!

Charlie had had enough of being pushed around. He went once again to the attorney general to complain. He was upheld. But it was too late for that year. The next year there was more pressure applied to the Vintage, this time from television. When word got out that Mike Wallace of CBS wanted to talk to Charlie about the tournament and the way he was treated, the Vintage promised Charlie an invitation if he refused the interview. Charlie turned down the interview and played the tournament.

Despite the setbacks and frustrations, things had begun to improve financially for Charlie. By 1980, the Seniors Tour was now an ongoing event, with big money and players his own age to compete against. Charlie's winnings increased. He was finally able to leave his job in Ohio and concentrate on his game again. By the late 1980s, he had made over a million dollars in golf, most of it on the Seniors Tour. And after all these years, he finally got an endorsement. The automobile maker Toyota was proud to have Charlie Sifford talk about its cars in advertisements. It looked like Charlie could relax at last and be able to compete fairly and frequently in the game he loved to play. But, as was so often the case in Charlie's life, things were not always how they seemed to be at first glance.

Chapter Seven

After Charlie left the clubhouse job at the Sleepy Hollow Country Club, he moved to Texas, near Houston. The money earned on the Seniors Tour allowed him to buy a nice home and to become a member of a local country club. Charlie was finally gaining the benefit of his years of struggle.

This did not mean that the struggle was over, however. At the 1986 Johnny Mathis Seniors Classic there was a new car plus an $100,000 prize to any player to make a hole-in-one. After Charlie made a hole-in-one, tournament officials said that announcing the prizes had been a mistake. They refused to pay him the money. Charlie had to sue and wait nearly two years before the tournament gave him the money and the car.

It was not until the 1990s that intense focus was placed on professional golf for the way it dealt with race relations. In 1990, the Shoal Creek Country Club in Alabama was chosen to host the PGA Championship. It was announced in the media that the club would not allow African Americans to join. When he was asked about the policy, the club's founder told the press: "We don't discriminate in any area but the blacks." Finally, after all the years that golfers like Charlie Sifford had struggled, public reaction was so severe that the PGA was forced to take action. It threatened to move the tournament if the club did not change its rules. The club quickly admitted a black man, although he had not played golf in twenty years.

The incident focused the nation's attention on the problems in golf that Charlie and other African Americans had been fighting against for decades. What was surprising was how the PGA acted as though it was shocked to discover that the country club discriminated against non-whites. Many of the clubs that sponsored PGA tournaments had only one or two non-white members. But the Shoal Creek incident did focus national attention on the problem. It would grow more and more difficult for professional golf to return to its old ways of running tournaments.

Charlie retired from active play after the 1995 season. When asked why he was leaving the game he loved, Charlie answered that he was too old to win. Why play if he had no chance of beating younger men? Since his boyhood at the Carolina Country Club in Charlotte, Charlie had been a fierce competitor. It was this drive that would not let him settle for less than the best when he began breaking into golf. If he did not have chances to beat the best in the sport, why even bother to play?

In April of 1997, Tiger Woods won the Masters, becoming the first African American ever to do so. He has acknowledged a debt to Charlie Sifford for opening the doors for him and calls Charlie his "honorary grandfather."

Maybe professional golf is finally changing and will acknowledge the contributions made by its pioneers of all colors. Maybe some day there will be as many warm words said about Charlie Sifford, Teddy Rhodes, and Lee Elder as there are about Byron Nelson, Bobby Jones, Arnold Palmer, or Jack Nicklaus. Only time will tell.

One thing is certain. Charlie Sifford will not sit around waiting for praises to come his way. He will continue speaking out on what he thinks is right. He blazed a trail in golf for others of his race to follow. He paid a price for his efforts. He's won some money, but not nearly as much as he could have won if he had been allowed to play in the big-money tournaments when he was younger. He still plays occasionally on the Seniors Tour, where his earnings have now gone over the two million mark.

For years, people referred to Charlie as the "Jackie Robinson of golf." He was always quick to point out that when Jackie Robinson broke the so-called "color-barrier" in baseball he had a team and its organization backing him up. All Charlie ever had was a golf club and the determination to not be kept away from the sport he loved and excelled at playing. But most importantly, Charlie had a dream, which he never stopped believing in, no matter what the world threw at him. His way was to believe in himself,

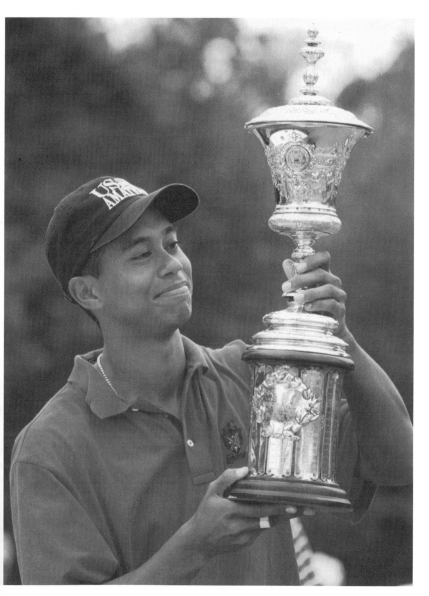

Tiger Woods calls Charlie Sifford his "honorary grandfather" and credits him with opening the doors to professional golf for non-white players.

to work hard, and to persist in the face of long odds and cruelty. In the end, this strategy worked for Charlie Sifford. Not only did he have a successful career; he improved the game of golf forever.

GLOSSARY

approach shot: shot intended to reach the green.

birdie: score of one shot under par for a single hole.

bogey: score of one shot over par on a single hole. A *double bogey* is a score of two shots over par on a single hole; *triple bogey* three.

caddie: person who carries a players bags and offers advice.

chip: a short, low shot, often used to get onto the green.

dogleg: a hole with a fairway angled away from the tee.

drive: shot from the tee.

eagle: score of two shots under par on a single hole.

fairway: grass between the tee and the green.

green: area of course designed for putting.

hole-in-one: hitting the tee shot into the hole.

match play: a competition decided by matching scores on individual holes.

medal play: a competition decided by the total number of strokes needed to complete a course.

par: score a player is expected to make at individual holes and courses.

PGA: Professional Golfer's Association.

putt: shot made on a green using a putter.

sudden death: a play-off to break a tie.

tee: area where a player begins to play a hole.

waggle: movement of hands and clubhead when positioning to hit the ball.

Bibliography

Barkow, Al. *Golf's Golden Grind: the History of the Tour*. New York: Harcourt Brace Jovanovich, 1974.

Dailey, John. *L.A. Sentinel* "Divot Diggings: Remembrance of the Sixties," V.LX; No. 47, 3-01-95.

Graffis, Herb. *The PGA*. New York: Thomas Y. Crowell, 1975.

Hershey, Steve. *The Senior Tour*. New York: Doubleday, 1992.

Keane, Christopher. *The Tour*. New York: Stein & Day, 1974.

Lacy, Tim. Afro-American @Lacy Sports http://afroam.org/information/lacy/lacy6-22-96 html/#L2.

Murray, Jack. *Detroit News*. "Sifford, 73, Still A Man With A Cause."

Robinson, Bob. *The Oregonian*. "A Question Of Color." Vol. 3, Article 94, 8-5-90.

Sifford, Charlie with Gullo, James. *Just Let Me Play*. New York. British American Publishing, 1992.

Black Enterprise. "Teeing Off: History of Blacks in Golf." V.25; No. 2; 9/94.

Index

NORTH SHORE · 08